I0616139

Investing in Silver

Investing in Silver

Bare-Bones Basics

Shelley Kuziak

Copyright © 2025 by Shelley Kuziak

All rights reserved. No part of this publication may be reproduced, distributed, or transmitted in any form or by any means without the prior written permission of the publisher, except in the case of brief quotations embodied in critical reviews and certain other noncommercial uses permitted by copyright law. email: SeshatBooks@gmail.com

The author is not a licensed investment advisor.

This book shares ideas about investing based on what has worked well in the past, and these ideas may or may not work well in the future. This is not personal financial advice. Talk to a money expert for help with investment choices. Although the author has made every effort to ensure that the information in this book was correct at press time, the author does not assume and hereby disclaim any liability to any party for any loss, damage, or disruption caused by errors or omissions, whether such errors or omissions result from negligence, accident, or any other cause.

ISBN: 979-8-218-71709-4

Front cover image by Michael Edwards Design
Printed in the United States of America
First paperback edition 2025

Table of Contents

Introduction

The Roaring Twenties ended with economic hardship, and times are no better in the 2020s:

1929 - The stock market crashed and by 1932, stocks had lost nearly 90% of their value.
2022 - The wildly profitable crypto market dropped in value by over 1 trillion dollars.
2025 - A one-day loss of $2.4 trillion in S&P 500 market value was recorded on April 3. (The Standard & Poor's 500 is a stock market index that tracks the performance of 500 leading companies listed on stock exchanges in the United States.)

INVEST IN SILVER TO RETAIN YOUR WEALTH.

Physical silver is an excellent investment:
- Many industries need silver to make their products so there is always a demand for it.
- Silver has had fundamental value for thousands of years. This will not change.
- Silver stacking can be 'strictly business,' such as a monthly coin purchase, or a "treasure hunt" for rare coins, novelty pieces, or any type of silver you desire.
- There is an abundance of products from which to choose regardless of your budget.

PATIENCE IS THE KEY TO BECOMING A SUCCESSFUL SILVER STACKER.

In January 2023, the market value of one ounce of silver was about $24.00. In January 2025, the price topped $30.00. In 1980 and 2011, investors had an opportunity to sell an ounce of silver for $50.00, an amount that financial analysts predict will be surpassed in the near future. So you may be able to increase your wealth, not just retain it, and this speculation is part of the fun of collecting silver.

However, silver is a volatile market, liable to change rapidly and unpredictably. Thus, there's always a possibility that your precious metals collection will be worth less when you sell it than when you acquired it. Adhere to the age-old investment philosophy - "buy low, sell high," and you can do well in this market. Selling opportunities are numerous when you feel the time is right.

Experts also predict that a bear market, a time marked by investment losses, will begin soon and persist for years. Further, a bear market is often an indicator that the U.S. economy is in a recession. It's been proven repeatedly that it's easier to make it through tough times when you own silver.

"In a bear market, he who loses least, wins." — Leon Cooperman, billionaire investor

Chapter 1

¤

Bullion and Coins

Bullion

Silver bullion is produced for investors. You have a choice between rounds or bars that almost always are 99.9% pure silver. Rounds look like coins, and they typically weigh one ounce. You can find numerous designs on bars and rounds, and there are more generic options available that feature a mint mark and purity level. In general, bullion rounds and bars offer the best value for investing in .999 pure silver.

Incuse Indian Silver Round   Asahi Refining Silver Round   Walking Liberty Silver Bar

(*Images Courtesy of Money Metals Exchange*)

Coins vs bullion

It's easy to differentiate between silver coins and bullion such as silver rounds. Silver coins have a face value, and they are
- legal tender.
- government-issued.
- guaranteed by the country that issued them.

Bullion coins

To clarify a somewhat confusing concept, the term "bullion coin" must be defined. A bullion coin is a legal tender product that has been produced based on the weight and purity of its precious metal content. So a bullion coin is mostly valued for its metal content rather than its condition or rarity. Therefore, this market primarily attracts investors instead of collectors. The American Silver Eagle is the official silver bullion coin of the USA.

Junk silver

Junk silver, or the nickels, dimes, quarters, half dollars, and dollars that were used in everyday commerce prior to 1965, was made of 90% pure silver. These old coins are also referred to as "constitutional silver," "90% silver," and "old US silver." In general, junk silver has no collectible value to numismatists. Silver coins, though, that pre-date the 1940s as well as rare coins minted later may have value to coin collectors.

While some vintage coin enthusiasts do not consider junk silver valuable, these coins are not junk! In fact, the U.S. Mint melted down many of the U.S. silver coins that were once in circulation. This includes 47% of all Morgan dollars minted between 1878 and 1904. So even though many millions of silver coins were once used for everyday transactions, relatively few remain today. Thus, junk silver is rare.

Services such as Professional Coin Grading Service (PCGS) and Numismatic Guaranty Corporation (NGC) can authenticate and grade circulated coins. These slabbed coins bring peace of mind to both investors and collectors. After grading, a coin is placed in a sealed, hard plastic holder (slab) that protects it from damage. A certification card is usually included.

Proof coins

Proof coins were once used to check the quality of a particular die before mass production of a coin began. Today, proof coins are minted for collectors. This finest type of coinage is struck twice rather than once like regular coins. Proof coins
- have a shiny, clean-looking finish.
- feature a well-defined and intricate design.

- include a protective case as well as official documentation to certify authenticity.

Uncirculated coins

Like proof coins, uncirculated coins do not have the wear or scratches that circulated coins usually have. But they are struck using the same method as regular circulated coins. According to the U.S. Mint, though, uncirculated coins have quality enhancements that include
- special packaging,
- early strikes from dies,
- slightly higher coining force,
- and special cleaning after stamping.

In summary, the U.S. Mint issues four types of coins - bullion coins made of precious metals, circulated and uncirculated coins, and proof coins. Fiat money, or the type of money produced throughout the latter years of the twentieth century and into the beginning years of the twenty-first century, is not backed by gold or silver. This means that the money you have in your pocket or wallet has no intrinsic value.

Spot price vs market price

The price of physical silver changes constantly. You can follow this ever-changing price on precious metals dealers' websites. Usually, dealers place the price at the top of the home page where it is easy to find. The amount listed is the spot price for one ounce of silver.

You pay the market price for silver coins and bullion when you purchase it, rather than the spot price. The market price includes a premium added to the spot price to cover costs associated with the acquiring and manufacturing of the metal, such as shipping, marketing, and customer service.

Paper silver

It's important to note that the term "physical silver" differentiates an item you hold in your hand from "paper silver." Exchange-traded funds (ETFs) and silver mining stocks are examples of paper silver. These financial instruments are tied to the performance of silver prices. They are not backed by physical silver.

A phrase commonly used by folks in the precious metals community is "if you don't hold it, you don't own it." So it is not surprising that many experts strongly caution silver stackers to research the pitfalls of paper silver before purchasing it. However, it is also noted that savvy silver stackers can increase their wealth by making prudent choices in the paper silver market.

Measurement

Precious metals, including silver, are measured in troy ounces. One troy ounce is equal to 1.097 standard ounces. So a troy ounce is equal to 31.1035 grams while a standard ounce is equal to 28.3495 grams. Thus, a troy ounce is about 10-percent heavier than a standard ounce. The troy ounce, a measurement that dates back to the Middle Ages, is used to ensure purity standards.

Chapter 2

¤

U.S. Minted Silver Coins

U.S. coins

As previously noted, junk silver refers to U.S. minted silver nickels, dimes, quarters, half dollars, and dollars. The time may come when you want to use junk silver to barter for goods and services. The following information about these old coins will help you with both investment and bartering decisions.

Jefferson war nickel

Jefferson War Nickel
(Image Courtesy of USA Coin Book)

Jefferson war nickels, like the nickels currently found in United States coinage, depict Thomas Jefferson on the obverse side and Monticello, Jefferson's estate in Virginia, on the reverse side.

The coins contained 35% silver, 56% copper, and 9% manganese. They were minted during World War II, or more precisely, from 1942 to 1945.

$1 face value of nickels = about 1.125 oz silver.
One roll of nickels contains about 2.25 oz silver.
The simplest calculation: 18 Jefferson war nickels = 1 oz silver (approximately)

Mercury/Roosevelt dime

Mercury Dime
(*Image Courtesy of USA Coin Book*)

Roosevelt dimes contained 90% silver and 10% copper during a period that extended from 1946 to 1964. This dime design was produced without silver after 1964. Mercury dimes struck by the U.S. Mint from late 1916 to 1945 have become a favorite of collectors.

The early-to-mid-twentieth-century dime depicts a lovely young Liberty. The headshot of this symbol of human freedom is notable because it shows off a winged conical cap with the apex bent over.

The reverse of the Mercury dime displays a fasces, or a bound bundle of wooden rods, a symbol of unity and strength. The fasces is wrapped with an olive branch that represents peace. These older dimes also contain 90% silver.

$1 face value of dimes = about 0.723 oz silver.
One roll of dimes contains about 3.575 oz silver.
The simplest calculation: 14 Mercury or Roosevelt dimes = 1 oz silver (approximately)

Washington quarter

Washington Quarter
(*Image Courtesy of USA Coin Book*)

A Washington quarter was made of copper and nickel beginning in 1965. Prior to this time, a quarter contained 90% silver and 10% copper. Shown on its obverse is the profile of George Washington, while its reverse features an eagle. Silver quarters are minted for proof sets such as the 50 state proof set.

5 Washington quarters = 1 oz silver (approximately)

Walking Liberty half dollar

Walking Liberty Half Dollar
(*Image Courtesy of USA Coin Book*)

Walking Liberty half dollars, or 'Walkers,' as they are known in the coin industry, were minted from 1916 to 1947. Walkers were not produced in 1922, 1924, 1925, 1926, 1930, 1931, or 1932. The coins are composed of 90% silver and 10% copper. They feature Lady Liberty, a rising sun, and the U.S. flag on the obverse and a bald eagle on the reverse.

Walking Liberty half dollars, considered to be one of the most beautiful U.S. coins ever minted, are popular with both silver and coin collectors.

3 Walking Liberty half dollars = 1 oz silver (approximately)

Franklin half dollar

Franklin Half Dollar
(*Image Courtesy of USA Coin Book*)

Beginning in 1948 and ending in 1963, the design on the half dollar coin featured a head and shoulders portrait of Founding Father Benjamin Franklin on the obverse and the Liberty Bell on the reverse.

A small eagle is to the right of the Liberty Bell, which meets the requirement of the Coinage Act of 1792 that an eagle appear on the reverse of all silver coins.

About 500 million of these 90% silver coins were minted for circulation over the years. With only 35 different dates and mint marks in the series, it is possible to assemble a rather inexpensive collection. Proof coins were minted from 1950 through 1963.

3 Franklin half dollars = 1 oz silver (approximately)

Kennedy Half Dollar

Kennedy Half Dollar
(*Image Courtesy of USA Coin Book*)

The Kennedy half dollar was struck from 90% silver when it was released in 1964. The obverse features a left profile of President Kennedy and the Presidential Seal appears on the reverse. From 1965 to 1970, each coin contained 40% silver and 60% copper. Any coin struck after 1970 contains no silver. Instead, coins have a nickel jacket over a copper core.

During 1975 and the bicentennial year 1976, an image of Independence Hall in Philadelphia was placed on the reverse. Production of half dollars ceased for general circulation after 2001 because of falling demand. But since 2002, half dollars have been minted for annual coin sets and other numismatic products.

3 Kennedy half dollars = 1 oz silver (approximately)

Morgan dollar

Morgan Dollar
(*Image Courtesy of USA Coin Book*)

The Morgan dollar, made of 90% silver, is one of the most highly collected U.S. coins. The obverse features a profile of Lady Liberty while the reverse shows an eagle with outstretched wings. The coin was minted from 1878 to 1904, and again in 1921. Modern Morgan dollars, made of 99.9% silver, were issued in 2021. Production began again in 2023.

A Morgan dollar contains 0.7734 oz silver.

Peace dollar

Peace Dollar
(*Image Courtesy of USA Coin Book*)

Coin and silver collectors also favor the Peace dollar. The obverse features a profile of Lady Liberty while the reverse shows a bald eagle clutching an olive branch. The 90% silver Peace dollar was minted from 1921 to 1935, and modern collectible Peace dollars, made of 99.9% silver, were issued in 2021. Production resumed in 2023.

A Peace dollar contains 0.7734 oz silver.

Eisenhower dollar

Eisenhower Dollar
(*Image Courtesy of USA Coin Book*)

In 1971, the Eisenhower dollar became the first dollar coin issued by the U.S. Mint since the Peace dollar series ended in 1935. The collectible coin contained 40% silver while the circulating coin held no silver. The coin marked two 1969 events: the passing of Dwight Eisenhower and the Apollo 11 moon landing. Thus, the reverse of the coin depicts the Apollo 11 mission insignia: a bald eagle landing on the moon. Production ended in 1978.

3 Eisenhower dollars = 1 oz silver (approximately)

American Silver Eagle

American Silver Eagle
(*Image Courtesy of USA Coin Book*)

The U.S. Mint launched the American Eagle Coin Program in 1986 with gold and silver bullion coins for investors. Platinum coins were added in 1997 while palladium coins were first released in 2017. The popular Walking Liberty design was revived for placement on the obverse. The original depiction of a bald eagle on the reverse was revamped in 2021.

American Silver Eagles contain one troy ounce of 99.9% pure silver. The weight and purity of each coin is guaranteed by the government. Bullion coins provide silver stackers with a convenient and cost effective way to buy physical silver a little at a time.

1 American Silver Eagle = 1 oz silver

American Silver Eagle Proof Coin

American Silver Eagle Proof Coin
(*Image Courtesy of the U.S. Mint*)

On August 20, 2025, the U.S. Mint issued its first laser-engraved coin. The American Silver Eagle Proof Coin features a unique privy mark inspired by the laser symbol that is used to indicate the use of laser-engraved technology. The attention-getting sunburst symbol is found on the obverse along with the full-length figure of Walking Liberty. The reverse design shows an eagle as it approaches a landing.

A total of 100,000 coins were struck at the Mint facility at West Point. This new laser-engraved technology guarantees extraordinary detail that produces a coin surface that has an almost three-dimensional look. And according to the mint, the technology will thwart counterfeiters, many of whom offer fake coins at unrealistic bargain prices on eBay and other online platforms.

Chapter 3

¤

Collections

Collecting coins

If you want to collect silver coins, there are many ways to assemble a collection, including these popular methods:

- date-and-mintmark set - each and every date and mintmark combination for a specific coin
- mintmark set - one coin from each mint that made it; choose one denomination or all silver coin designs produced.
- 1-year set - choose one year and one coin or one year and all types of silver coins produced that year.
- short set - each of the dates and mintmarks struck within a short range of years for one coin, in other words, a consecutive date range shorter than the span of the entire series.
- type set - all designs made for one denomination, such as the four types of nickels that the United States Mint has produced.
- proof set - proof coins of each denomination made in a year
- random coins that have personal meaning to the collector

Common denominations

1-ounce collector coins as well as 1-ounce rounds and bars are most commonly chosen by members of the physical silver collector community, but other denominations are available. Two-, five-, and ten-ounce silver products are a good addition to any collection. Stackers who have a larger amount of money to invest can purchase 50-ounce or 100-ounce bars. Budget-conscious investors appreciate 1/10-ounce rounds as well as 1/4-ounce and 1/2-ounce rounds.

American Silver Eagle Monster Box

The "holy grail," or the collectible that is most highly prized, for silver stackers is the American Silver Eagle Monster Box. Each sealed box contains 25 tubes of 20-count uncirculated 1-ounce American Silver Eagles for a total of 500 ounces of 0.999 fine silver. This is an ideal investment for anyone who is purchasing a large amount of physical silver since the U.S. Mint guarantees the box.

If you plan to purchase 500 Silver Eagles a few at a time, you can purchase an empty box and 25 tubes from the mint and create your own Monster Box. The green heavy-duty plastic box measures 15" x 8.5" x 4.5". It weighs about 3 pounds when empty and about 40 pounds when full.

Mini Monster Box

An American Silver Eagle Mini Monster Box, which contains 100 coins, is another option. Or choose a different coin or round. You can purchase a few pieces of silver at a time along with an empty box and 5 tubes if you want to assemble your own Mini Monster Box.

1 ounce Silver Buffalo Round Mini Monster Box

1 ounce Silver American Flag Bar Mini Monster Box
(*Images Courtesy of JM Bullion*)

Chapter 4

¤

One-of-a-kind Items

Novelty pieces

Creating a collection of novelty pieces makes collecting silver fun. While this type of silver is often more expensive per ounce than bars or rounds, like-minded buyers make it probable that each piece will hold its value.

Silver bullets, designed to look like various calibers, are a popular choice. Goldpanner divisible silver bars and interlocking, stackable silver eagle rounds are creative and out of the ordinary options. Sugar skulls, dice, zodiac signs, and building blocks are a few more of the many silver pieces that can enhance a collection.

9mm Hollow Point Bullet   Zodiac Sign Round
(*Images Courtesy of Money Metals Exchange*)

Goldpanner Divisible Silver Round
(*Images Courtesy of JM Bullion*)

Eagle Stacker   Dice
(*Image Courtesy of*   (*Image Courtesy*
Scottsdale Mint*)   of JM Bullion*)

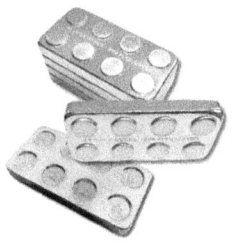

Sugar Skull   Building Blocks
(*Images Courtesy of Monarch Precious Metals*)

Chapter 5

¤

Sterling, Coin, and British Silver

Sterling silver

Jewelry, flatware, and decorative pieces such as candle holders can be made of sterling silver, which usually has a silver purity of 92.5%. Copper or another metal or mixture of metals is added. Since pure silver is soft, the inclusion of these metals gives the silver added strength and durability. If "925," "sterling," or "ster" is stamped on an item, it is sterling silver.

Since sterling silver includes at least two different metals, it is an alloy rather than a precious metal. Still, it has value. In fact, you may find that you can get quality items for a good price. Even damaged items, such as dented silverware, have value since the silver can be melted down, separated from other metals, and used to produce a new silver item. Many coin dealers buy sterling silver.

Coin silver

In the nineteenth-century, coins were often melted down to produce bowls, trays, flatware, goblets, and more. At the time, coins contained roughly 90% silver and 10% copper, and soon, any item made of this metal combination was called "coin silver." Vintage objects from this era were sometimes stamped "Coin," "Pure Coin," or "C." However, the silver content in U.S. coins changed more than once during the century.

British silver

Silver items made in Britain feature a hallmark that is mandated by law. Hallmarks, which date back to the Middle Ages, are a form of regulation and consumer protection. A hallmark includes a combination of marks that name the origin and age of each piece. Specifically, the hallmark can include the assay office symbol, the date letter, the maker's mark, and the standard/purity mark as well as a duty mark on items made between 1784 and 1890.

British Hallmark
(*Image Courtesy of www.silvercollection.it*)

Chapter 6

¤

Hedging, IRAs, and Silver Banking

Hedging

Silver stackers typically purchase bullion coins as a hedge against inflation. Hedging is a strategy that tries to limit risks in financial assets. Inflation hedging offsets an anticipated drop in a government-issued currency's price. The value of the U.S. dollar continues to trend downward in the 2020s, in contrast to physical silver.

To review, a sovereign government, such as the United States government, mints coins. All silver coins are legal tender that have a minimum face value in addition to a melt value and a possible collectible value. Private mints mint rounds and bars which have no face value and usually have only a melt value. Both silver coins and silver rounds can be used as a hedge against inflation.

IRS-approved precious metals

American Silver Eagles, as well as silver rounds and bars, are allowed in an individual retirement account (IRA). Gold, platinum, and palladium products can also be placed in an IRA. To receive

IRS approval, coins and bullion must be produced by an approved mint and meet the following criteria:

- gold - 99.5% pure
- silver - 99.9% pure
- platinum/palladium - 99.95% pure

According to the Gold IRA Guide, investors must make a minimum initial purchase of $5,000 of approved metals to establish a precious metals IRA, and each subsequent purchase must be at least $1,000. The metals must be stored in an IRS-approved depository, which is responsible for the safety and maintenance of the bullion it houses.

Simply put, precious metals that are in your personal possession cannot be placed into an IRA.

"Silver banking"

Consumers can satisfy their banking needs with options that were not available in the past. Battle Bank is an example of a bank that offers non-traditional lending and investing solutions. Battle Bank provides recession-resilient, high-yield offerings such as precious metals trading as well as lending on existing client metals holdings. Other options for financial freedom include market-linked Certificates of Deposit and self-directed IRAs.

Chapter 7

¤

Best Silver For Your Needs

Bad economic times

To summarize, you can collect a broad range of silver items or concentrate on a specific area or item. Remember that the most important reason for collecting physical silver is to retain your wealth, especially during bad economic times. Thus, when weighing the pros and cons of collecting each type of silver, keep in mind that fiat currency

- may be replaced by or supplemented with a new type of exchange. Because of rapidly changing technology, currency modification may even occur more than once in the near future. A Central Bank Digital Currency (CBDC) has been discussed by people who are in the know about financial issues.
- is backed only by trust in government. Thus, the value of fiat money can fluctuate significantly because of a range of political, economic, and psychological factors. High inflation is one of these factors.

Silver and other precious metals may become necessary for survival in the near future. A "black market" of sorts may be created if a CBDC is issued, meaning that you can barter for goods with like-minded folks in your community. While a CBDC may initially seem very convenient and easy to use, be aware that the government can track as well as control purchases you make if this type of currency becomes a reality.

It is also wise to consider your goals, or what you would most prefer to do with your silver if you're given the opportunity. You can use your silver collection in the following ways:

- to provide motivation to save money instead of "just wasting it on stuff."
- to buy income-producing property.
- in place of a savings account.
- to help a child or grandchild.
- for travel expenses.
- to make saving fun.
- for a big purchase.
- during retirement.

Think outside the box

A little creativity can serve you well when you are a silver stacker. Use this idea from Uneducated Economist* as a springboard for your own ideas. This popular YouTube influencer wanted to buy a truck that cost $3,000. He didn't have the money but he had silver.

The seller wanted to sell his truck, of course, but he didn't want silver. So the two men made a deal. The seller held the silver as collateral. At the end of the deal, Uneducated Economist got all of his silver back, and the seller got $3,300. (the price of the truck plus 10% interest)

Hope for the best economic times so you can sell or save your silver as you like, but be ready to use it to maintain a good standard of living during economic downturns.

Chapter 8

¤

Online Dealers

Precious metals dealers

APMEX offers the largest selection of products, but it's just one of many online precious metals dealers. Here are a few more companies that offer high-quality silver items: SD Bullion, JM Bullion, Monarch Precious Metals, Kinesis Bullion, Provident Metals, Money Metals Exchange, Bison Bullion, BGASC, Hero Bullion, Mile High Mint, Scottsdale Mint, The Perth Mint, New Zealand Mint, and Miles Franklin.

Buy from precious metals dealers

Expect an easy ordering process when you purchase silver bullion or coins from online precious metals dealers. Often, if the item you want to purchase is out of stock, you can be notified when it becomes available. Some dealers accept Bitcoin and other cryptocurrencies as well as checks, credit cards, and PayPal. There may be an upcharge that is dependent upon how much silver you buy and how you pay for it.

Here is an example:

Quantity	Check/Wire	Crypto	CC/PayPal
1-24	$30.00	$30.31	$31.25

Sell to precious metals dealers

Many precious metals dealers will buy your silver when you are ready to sell, regardless of where you purchased it originally. So if the price is right or if you have an emergency and need cash, you can sell some or all of your collection with little effort. Usually, a dealer lists a minimum purchase amount on the company website. When you call to get a buy-back price, the dealer locks in the price of your silver over the phone. Shipping instructions are provided.

Buy from the U.S. Mint

Official U.S. Mint products are available for sale at usmint.gov. You can also find fact-filled articles on the website. Sign up for a subscription, and you will automatically receive the next product in a coin series of your choice. The U.S. Mint also offers a monthly newsletter, Loyalty Program, and emails or texts with product or promotion updates.

Chapter 9

¤

More Budget-Friendly Options

Copper

"A penny saved is two pennies clear." — Benjamin Franklin

Franklin used this quote to convey that a life of thrift is best. So if you don't spend a penny and save it instead, you're "up" a penny instead of "down" a penny and thus, twice as rich. A penny saved actually is two pennies clear (or more) if you save copper Lincoln pennies.

Pennies minted between 1959 and early 1962 contain 95-percent copper and 5-percent tin and zinc. Tin was not part of the composition from late 1962 to 1982, but the amount of copper remained the same. In October 1982, composition of the one-cent coin changed to 97.5-percent zinc and 2.5-percent copper.

More precisely, copper plating covered the zinc coin to preserve the penny's appearance. Since both copper and zinc pennies were produced in 1982, you need to determine the primary metal when you acquire a penny minted in this year.

- A copper penny weighs 3.11 grams, and a zinc penny weighs 2.5 grams.
- When dropped on a hard surface, a copper penny "rings" while a zinc penny "clicks."
- Most of the time, a worn copper penny has a chocolate brown appearance while a zinc penny displays an uneven toning.

Some wheat pennies, minted between 1909 and 1958, remained in circulation for decades so "penny savers" may be able to find some in their collection. Pre-1983 pennies are available for purchase. Precious metals dealers sell 50-count rolls of copper pennies as well as 5,000 coin bags. ($50.00 face value) Copper, like silver, is a metal that will likely increase in price in coming years.

Goldback

Goldback
(*Image Courtesy of Money Metals Exchange*)

As noted on goldback.com, a Goldback is "physical, interchangeable, gold money that is designed to accommodate even small transactions." The intent of this program, which launched in 2019, is to encourage people to circulate physical gold, as has been done in the past. Many precious metals dealers, including Money Metals Exchange and JM Bullion, sell this gold paper currency.

The most recent technology makes it possible to produce Goldbacks. This colorful, visually attractive currency features atomized 24-karat gold particles. One Goldback contains 1/1,000th of an ounce of 24-karat gold while a Fifty Goldback contains 50 times that, or 1/20th of an ounce. State series are produced, and each series includes 1, 5, 10, 25, and 50 denominations.

This unique program, which aims to honor each state in the USA, is a work in progress. Florida, Utah, Nevada, New Hampshire, South Dakota, and Wyoming Goldbacks were the first to be released. While many small businesses accept this paper gold, major retailers do not. It's a great collector's item, and you may want to collect each "bill" that has been produced.

Precious metals mining stocks

In the past, middle-class investors increased their investment dollars substantially by putting their money in silver and other precious metals mining stocks. But these stocks are risky investments so you should never invest money that you can't afford to lose. As with physical silver and most other types of investments, you are most likely to find success with stocks if you use the "buy low, sell high" strategy.

Again, it is possible to realize life-changing returns by investing a relatively small amount of money if you make smart investment decisions. If your primary income covers your bills and not much more, it may be worth your time and effort to get a side gig so you have money to invest. Keep in mind, though, that a huge amount of research is also necessary if you want to make good investment choices. But online resources make this research easy to do.

Chapter 10

¤

Expand Your Knowledge

Additional research

Currently, the USA as well as the rest of the world is going through tough economic times, and this is unlikely to change in the foreseeable future. The more you understand about topics related to silver stacking, the more likely you are to thrive at a time when others are struggling.

You may want to do further research on economic topics like yield curve inversion, inflation, and supply and demand as well as historical events like the removal of the gold standard, the 1929 stock market crash, and the Hunt brothers cornering of the silver market in the 1970s.

You can easily learn about topics relevant to silver stacking by watching podcasts online. Podcast hosts interview experts in the financial and economic sectors who have exceptional knowledge about the silver market. These experts often provide websites or newsletters packed with helpful information. Undoubtedly, you will find podcasts that you like, and you can follow them regularly.

To get you started on your quest for practical information, here are a few YouTube podcasts: ITM Trading, David Lin, The Jay Martin Show, Liberty and Finance, Natural Resource Stocks, Palisades Gold Radio, Thoughtful Money, Investing News, Commodity Culture, CapitalCosm, and Soar Financially.* The information provided is useful to both new and long-time investors.

Popular interviewees include Rick Rule, Stephanie Pomboy, Craig Hemke, Michael Pento, Mike Maloney, David Morgan, Bill Holter, Andy Schectman, Jeff Clark, John Rubino, and Peter Grandich.* These financial gurus are well-regarded by their peers as well as YouTube viewers. Many silver aficionados find that the experts' insights help them create a wise investment strategy.

*The author does not endorse nor is affiliated with any entity (person or podcast) listed in this book. The author receives no remuneration from any of these entities.

Chapter 11

¤

Money and Precious Metals

Silver and gold are money again

"As a precious metal, silver is also money." —
Robert Kiyosaki, author of the Rich Dad, Poor Dad
series of personal finance books

In May 2025, silver and gold became money again
in Florida with the passage of CS/HB 999. More
specifically, the bill recognizes gold and silver as
legal tender for everyday transactions. As listed on
the Florida House of Representatives website: "The
purpose of this bill is to define and enact the
constitutional right to declare gold and silver as
legal tender, eliminate the tax burden, and make it
a functional means of transaction between willing
parties."

According to Daniel Diaz, Executive Director of
Citizens for Sound Money, this bill is the most
comprehensive sound money legislation for the
electronic transfer of gold and silver as legal tender.
When speaking about the bill, Mr. Diaz notes that
Florida has created legislation that is a model for
the rest of the country. That is good news for silver

stackers who are likely to find new and exciting financial opportunities.

Summary

Physical silver is a smart investment, especially in years of uncertainty. A rich variety of silver coins and bullion are readily available and enthusiastic buyers and sellers create a stress-free investment environment. Join the silver stacker community, and it won't take long to become hooked on collecting this shiny "treasure."

Glossary

Assay - lab test that determines the precise content and quality of a precious metal

Bullion - any 99.9% pure silver bar or round that gets its value solely from its metal content

Cull coin - worst grade of coin, but intrinsic value is retained despite its poor condition

Fiat money - government-issued currency that is not backed by gold or silver

Junk silver - U.S. nickels, dimes, quarters, half dollars, and dollars that were minted before 1965

Market price - price the customer pays for silver

Mintmark - small mark stamped into a coin to identify the mint that produced it

Numismatics - collection or study of currency, including coins

Numismatist - a very well-informed collector of coins or a scholar/dealer who researches the world of money from a cultural, historic, or artistic sense

Obverse (of a coin) - commonly called "heads" because it often depicts the head of a prominent person

Privy Mark - small design or symbol added to a coin for multiple purposes, including to identify its origin or to commemorate an event

Reverse (of a coin) - commonly called "tails"

Round - coin-like 99.9% pure silver bullion that is not legal tender issued by a government

Security chip - authenticating feature that is embedded in slabbed coins to retain information like the certification number, date, and mintmark

Silver stacker - person who invests in physical silver for the long term

Slabbed coin - certified coin that has been authenticated, graded, and placed in a hard, plastic holder (slab) by a professional grading service

Spot price - current price of silver in the precious metals marketplace

www.ingramcontent.com/pod-product-compliance
Lightning Source LLC
Chambersburg PA
CBHW071546120626
46550CB00006B/2595